Golden Delicious

This Package Contains

GOLDEN DELICIOUS
QUEEN OF
ALL GOLDEN APPLES
Trade Mark Reg.

For _____
_____
_____

From--- **Stark Bro's N. & O. Co.**
Louisiana, Missouri

MERCHANDISE---FOURTH CLASS MAIL

"Postmaster"--This Parcel may be opened for Inspection

A Cinderella Apple Story

Anna Egan Smucker

Illustrated by **Kathleen Kemly**

Albert Whitman & Company, Morton Grove, Illinois

*I*t was apple season in the fall of 1905, and the Stark Bro's Nursery in Louisiana, Missouri, was flooded with apples. They were sent by farmers who hoped they had grown the world's best *new* apple, one the Stark brothers would want to sell to all their customers.

"I feel like the prince who tried a glass slipper on one smelly foot after another to find Cinderella," Paul Stark said to his brother, Lloyd. Paul had just tasted another disappointing apple that sure had looked like royalty.

But all those disappointments didn't stop the Stark brothers from dreaming about finding the perfect apple, one that could be crowned Queen of the Apple World and bring them fame . . . and fortune.

Meanwhile, miles and miles away in the hills of West Virginia, Anderson Mullins was inspecting his new farm. It had been a hot summer, and everything was dry as dust.

He hadn't reckoned on coming face to face
with a miracle. "Holy cow!" he exclaimed. There,
in the midst of his dried-up apple orchard, was
a glorious, green-leaved tree, its branches loaded
with shining golden apples.

He snapped one off and took a bite. Never had he tasted
an apple so sweet, so juicy, so gosh-darned DELICIOUS!

For the next eight years, during wet seasons and dry seasons, Anderson Mullins's tree produced bushels and bushels of those golden apples. Every time he entered them in the Clay County fair, they won blue ribbons.

Each year, his tree produced fruit when other trees didn't. Come springtime, when the other apples that had been in his fruit cellar all winter were wrinkly and dried-out, his golden apples were still fresh and sweet. He was sure they were like no other apples in the whole wide world.

So, in the spring of 1914, Anderson Mullins searched his fruit cellar for the three most perfect golden apples he could find and sent them to the Stark Bro's Nursery. He knew the Starks were always on the lookout for new and better kinds of fruit, and he was hoping for some extra dollars in his pocket.

By and by, the apples arrived.

"Mullins' Yellow Seedling samples," Paul Stark read, blowing sawdust off the card.

"Don't waste your time on them," his brother Lloyd muttered. "Yellow apples don't sell. Tough skin, bland taste, and they don't keep well."

But Paul had just bitten into a slice. "Lloyd . . . Lloyd!" he yelled. And he shoved a piece in his brother's mouth. "Taste . . . taste this!"

"Mmmmm . . . juicy!" said Lloyd.

"Crisp and spicy!" said Paul. "Even though it's at least six months old!"

"This can't be a yellow apple!" Lloyd exclaimed.

"It's not," said Paul, his smile bigger than a giant slice of watermelon. "It's not a yellow apple. It's a GOLDEN apple!"

"This just might be our Cinderella!" shouted Lloyd.

Paul Stark found it hard to wait till the next apple harvest
season. When fall finally came, he traveled hundreds of miles to
see that golden apple tree. First by train and then by horseback
over winding mountain roads, he reached Odessa, West Virginia.

The sun poured down hot as apple butter just out of the kettle. His white shirt stuck to him tighter than the skin on a grape, but he didn't care.

At last, on a dusty country road along Porter's Creek
near Odessa, Paul saw a mailbox that said "A. H. Mullins."
He knew his journey was almost at an end.

No one answered when he knocked on the door, so he set out on his own to find Mullins's orchard and its extraordinary tree.

Paul wasn't used to hills as steep as those in Clay County, West Virginia. Sweating and gasping for breath, he climbed and climbed. At first, he found only some scraggly old trees. But then he saw it—a tree with rich green leaves, its branches bent to the ground with the weight of a great crop of gorgeous, glowing, golden apples.

Paul couldn't help himself. It was as if his hand reached out by itself and plucked one.

He was biting into it when a farmer came striding down the hill
toward him.

"My name's Paul Stark," Paul told the farmer. "That's some apple!"

"Name's Mullins," the farmer said. "I sent you some."

"I know," Paul said. "And I'd like to buy that tree from you."

So the two men put their heads together and agreed on a price.

Paul Stark hired workmen to build a cage to protect the tree from animals and thieves. He even ordered a wire strung from the locked cage to a battery-powered burglar alarm in Anderson Mullins's kitchen.

When Paul Stark left Mullins's farm, he took a bundle of twigs from the golden apple tree with him. In early spring, those twigs were grafted onto some of the Stark brothers' apple trees—cut into the stems and wrapped tight so the two would grow together. Paul and Lloyd watched over them as if those grafted trees were hens getting ready to lay golden eggs.

Those young trees grew quickly. It wasn't long before beautiful golden apples filled their branches.

And what did Paul and Lloyd Stark name their apples?
That was easy—GOLDEN DELICIOUS!

In 1919, Golden Delicious won a medal for the world's best new apple. You might say it was crowned queen—Queen of the Apple World!

This story is true. Golden Delicious apples made their first appearance on a tree "that just grew" on Anderson Mullins's farm in Clay County, West Virginia. After Paul and Lloyd Stark of the Stark Bro's Nurseries & Orchards Co. sampled one of these extraordinary apples in 1914, the rest became history.

Paul Stark was always looking for new varieties of fruit that could add to the profits of his nursery. When a customer reported, or sent, a fruit that seemed new and different, Paul was ready to travel any distance to see the tree.

Sprouted by chance around 1900, the Golden Delicious tree lived until the late 1950s, producing beautiful apples for most of its long life. Apple experts say that it was the happy result of a Golden Reinette apple pollinated by the Grimes Golden apple. The Grimes Golden, another apple discovered in West Virginia, was possibly planted by John Chapman, a man most of us know as Johnny Appleseed.

Just as children are not exact copies of their parents, an apple's seeds will not grow into trees bearing exactly the same kind of fruit as the "parent." Therefore, when someone wants to grow a certain kind of apple, twigs of that apple's "parent" tree, called *scions* (SY-uhns), are grafted onto another very small tree, called the *rootstock*. In this process, pieces of both trees are slit to expose their *cambium,* a layer of living cells that take up water and nutrients. These slits are fitted together like a puzzle and wrapped tightly so the two will grow together. The scions contain buds from which branches and leaves will grow into a tree that is identical to the "parent" tree. The rootstock provides the root system for the new plant.

Like the Golden Delicious, most varieties of apples are the result of chance. A tree grows from a seed that results from the blossom of one tree being pollinated by the pollen of another tree. It is no wonder that there are about seventy-five hundred kinds of apples in the world! Scientific experiments that carefully control pollination, along with years of research observing the characteristics of new trees, are the other way apple varieties are created. The new varieties are then grown by grafting. An example is the Fuji apple. It was developed in 1939 by Japanese breeders who crossed the Red Delicious apple with the Ralls Genet.

When the Stark brothers' trees began producing their own golden apples, by way of the grafting process, Paul and Lloyd needed a name for their new apple. It made both good sense and good *cents* to name it "Golden Delicious," a name that connected it to their best-selling Red Delicious apple. The Stark Bro's Nurseries & Orchards Co., founded in 1816, still exists and is one of the oldest nurseries in the United States.

In 1919, the Golden Delicious was awarded the Wilder Medal of the American Pomological Society. It is the only yellow apple to receive this "Nobel Prize" of the apple world. In 1995, the Golden Delicious was named the state fruit of West Virginia. Every fall, Clay County, West Virginia, where the Golden Delicious first sprouted, celebrates with the Clay County Golden Delicious Festival. In the festival's first year, a huge pie was baked, measuring six feet across and filled with sweet, juicy Golden Delicious apples.

Each year, billions of pounds of Golden Delicious apples are harvested throughout the world. Every one of those apples is a descendant of the tree Anderson Mullins found growing in his hillside orchard over a hundred years ago.

For my grandsons Daniel and Aaron.—A.E.S.

For the talented and wonderful painters of Bumping Lake—Jo, Gudrun, Isobel, Michelle, Rebecca, Sarah, Suzy, and last but not least, Tara.—K.K.

Special thanks to Larry Campbell, West Virginia University Harrison County Extension Agent, for his help in understanding the grafting process; John L. Marra, West Virginia University Cabell County Extension Agent, for writing about the discovery of the Golden Delicious apple in "The Greatest Apple in the World: Striking Gold in the Clay County Hills," published in *Goldenseal* 21, No. 3 (Fall 1995); and Adrian Ettlinger for determining the railroad route taken by Paul Stark.

Library of Congress Cataloging-in-Publication Data

Smucker, Anna Egan.
Golden delicious : a Cinderella apple story / by Anna Egan Smucker ; illustrated by Kathleen Kemly.
p. cm.
ISBN 978-0-8075-2987-4
1. Apples—Juvenile literature. 2. Apples—Varieties—United States—Juvenile literature. I. Title.
SB363.3.G65S68 2008 634'.11—dc22 2007052792

The design is by Carol Gildar.

For more information about Albert Whitman & Company, please visit our web site at www.albertwhitman.com.

The trade names "Stark Bro's Nurseries & Orchards Co.," Stark Bro's, and trademarked logos are used by permission of Stark Bro's Nurseries & Orchards Co., Louisiana, MO.

The package label on the title page is Courtesy of the Missouri State Archives, Trademark Collection.